Kabiko Talks about...
Children's Rights

By

Tulia Lopes

December 2013

This little book wishes to honor all children around the world, and their rights to a fair and decent life.

It is specially dedicated to my wonderful and gorgeous niece and nephew, Isadora and Ciro.

Love you!

Tulia

Article #1

We have the right to work together in peace to defend our rights.

Article #2

We are all born free.

Children have the right of expressing their own thoughts and ideas.

Article #4

Every child should be
treated the same way.

Article #5

Children should be cared for
and not be neglected.

Article #6

Children should be protected against labour and exploitation.

Article #7

Children should be protected against any form of violence and abuse.

Article #8

Children have the right of equality and to be protected by law.

Article #9

Children who break the law should receive legal help and rehabilitation.

My name is Kabiko.

Article #10
Children have the right to a
legally registered name.

Children have the right to feel protected in their own environment.

Article #12

Children have the right to belong to a country and have a nationality.

Children have the right to their childhood, love and friendship.

Article #14

Children have the right to believe
in what they like.

Article #15

Children have the right to share their ideas with others.

Article #16

Children have the right to a home where they are properly cared for.

Article #17

Every child has the right
for education.

Article #18

Education should allow children to develop their talents to the fullest.

Music, art, craft, and sport are for everyone to enjoy.

Article #20

All children have the right
to relax and play.

Article #21

Children have the right to live in a spirit of peace, dignity and tolerance.

Article #22

Mothers and children have the right to have access to health care.

Article #23

Every child has the right to a job,
and to a fair wage when grown-up.

Article #24

Nobody can take away these rights and freedoms from us.

Article #25

These rights should be available to all children around the world.

Kabiko and his Tribe are the characters created to support and promote **Kabiko Depot,** an online Buy & Sell platform where a percentage of every sale goes to the charities supported through the website.

When you buy this book you are helping us to help children around the world. A percentage of every purchase will be donated to the charities we support. Visit www.kabiko.com for more information.

The content of this book was inspired by the "Universal Declaration of Human Rights by United Nations."

Thank you for your purchase and we hope you and your family enjoy it!

KABIKO DEPOT
helping children in every sale you make

www.ingramcontent.com/pod-product-compliance
Lightning Source LLC
Chambersburg PA
CBHW042118040426

42449CB00002B/88